SUPER-AWESOME SCIENCE

THE SCIENCE OF
DINOSAURS

by Kathryn Hulick

Content Consultant
David A. Burnham, PhD
Preparator
Biodiversity Institute at the University of Kansas

Core Library

An Imprint of Abdo Publishing
abdopublishing.com

abdopublishing.com

Published by Abdo Publishing, a division of ABDO, PO Box 398166, Minneapolis, Minnesota 55439. Copyright © 2017 by Abdo Consulting Group, Inc. International copyrights reserved in all countries. No part of this book may be reproduced in any form without written permission from the publisher. Core Library™ is a trademark and logo of Abdo Publishing.

Printed in the United States of America, North Mankato, Minnesota
042016
092016

THIS BOOK CONTAINS
RECYCLED MATERIALS

Cover Photo: Jianying Yin/Shutterstock Images
Interior Photos: Jianying Yin/Shutterstock Images, 1; Piero Oliosi/Polaris/Newscom, 4, 6; Jennifer Borton/iStockphoto, 9; Roger Harris/Science Source, 11, 43; Sergey Krasovskiy/Stocktrek Images/Corbis, 12; Leonello Calvetti/Stocktrek Images/Corbis, 14; Shutterstock Images, 17 (background), 17 (middle background), 17 (middle foreground), 17 (foreground); iStockphoto, 17 (left); Kerry Huller/Casper Star-Tribune/AP Images, 18; Daniel Eskridge/Stocktrek Images/Corbis, 20, 45; Andreas Meyer/Shutterstock Images, 23; Mohamad Haghani/Stocktrek Images/Corbis, 26; Mark Stevenson/Stocktrek Images/Corbis, 29, 31; Mark Garlick/Science Photo Library/Newscom, 34, 40; Sebastian Kaulitzki/Shutterstock Images, 36; Jan Sovak/Stocktrek Images/Corbis, 38

Editor: Jon Westmark
Series Designer: Jake Nordby

Publisher's Cataloging in Publication Data
Names: Hulick, Kathryn, author.
Title: The science of dinosaurs / by Kathryn Hulick.
Description: Minneapolis, MN : Abdo Publishing, [2017] | Series: Super-awesome
     science | Includes bibliographical references and index.
Identifiers: LCCN 2015960500 | ISBN 9781680782462 (lib. bdg.) |
     ISBN 9781680776577 (ebook)
Subjects: LCSH: Dinosaurs--Juvenile literature.
Classification: DDC 567.9--dc23
LC record available at http://lccn.loc.gov/2015960500

CONTENTS

CHAPTER ONE

DINOSAUR WORLD

A massive *Spinosaurus* floats along an ancient river. The 50-foot (15-m) creature resembles a giant crocodile with a large sail on its back. As it stalks its prey through the water, the sail rises six feet (1.8 m) above the surface. A fish tries to dart away from the dinosaur. The *Spinosaurus* uses its paddle-like feet to lunge forward. The fish disappears into the dinosaur's wide snout.

Spinosaurus is the largest known meat-eating dinosaur.

Based on its body proportions, scientists believe *Spinosaurus* lived in the water.

It may sound as if this is a scene from a movie. But *Spinosaurus* was real. It is the earliest known swimming dinosaur, and it lived in the waters of northern Africa 97 million years ago.

How do we know these things? No person has ever seen a *Spinosaurus* in real life. But these creatures left behind bones, eggs, and footprints. Some of these things formed into fossils. A fossil by itself looks like a funny-shaped rock. But fossils contain secrets. To reveal those secrets, we use science. Scientists can discover which animal formed a fossil and how that animal lived.

Science provides a window into the past. It allows us to learn about animals that died tens of millions of years ago. Dinosaur science is part of a discipline called

IN THE REAL WORLD
A Fossil Birthday Cake

As layers of dirt, sand, and debris collect on the ground, the old ground gets covered up. Over millions of years, heat and pressure turn the old ground into rock. Sometimes animals or plants that died and fell to the ground also get covered up and become fossils. The rocks and fossils form a stack of layers, called strata. At the Blue Nile Gorge site in Ethiopia, the Nile River cut through these strata, like someone slicing into a birthday cake. Scientists have found fish scales, pieces of turtle shells, and dinosaur teeth. The layer a fossil comes from reveals the time period in which that animal lived and died.

paleontology, and the people who study dinosaurs are paleontologists.

A Dinosaur Time Machine

Imagine a time machine could take you back to see your favorite dinosaurs. You would have to take many separate trips to see all of them. Dinosaurs roamed Earth for a very, very long time—185 million years. During this time span, many new dinosaurs appeared. They evolved from earlier animals. Some of these new dinosaurs eventually died out. Others evolved into even more new forms. Other creatures, including giant sharks, early birds, and small mammals, shared the planet with the dinosaurs.

Scientists divide up Earth's history into chunks of time. The time of the dinosaurs is called the Mesozoic era. It contains three smaller chunks: the Triassic, Jurassic, and Cretaceous periods. The Mesozoic era came to an end about 66 million years ago, when approximately half of all species on the planet went extinct. To understand how long dinosaurs ruled,

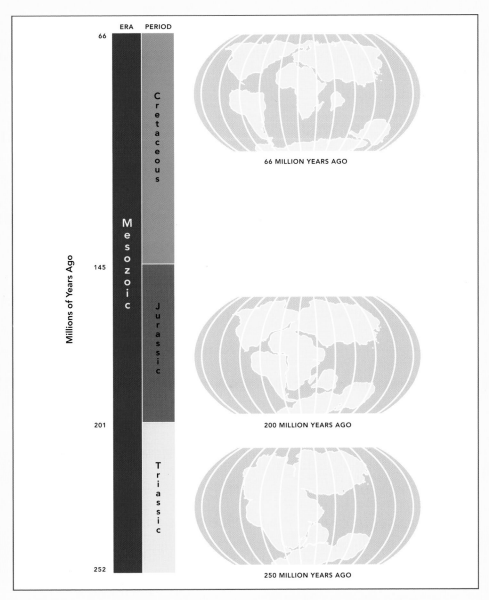

ERA   PERIOD

66

Cretaceous

66 MILLION YEARS AGO

Mesozoic

Millions of Years Ago

145

Jurassic

200 MILLION YEARS AGO

201

Triassic

250 MILLION YEARS AGO

252

A Changing World

Scientists divide the Mesozoic era into three chunks of time, called the Triassic, Jurassic, and Cretaceous periods. At the beginning of the Mesozoic era, all of the continents were squashed together into one giant landmass, called Pangaea. Slowly they moved apart to where they are now. How has the land shifted from the end of the Mesozoic era to today?

imagine that life on Earth started one hour ago. Dinosaurs would have appeared about half an hour ago. Then they would have died out about 19 minutes later. Humans, however, would have shown up only in the last six seconds of the hour!

Long, Long Ago

It might be fun to imagine a ferocious *Tyrannosaurus rex* battling a spiny *Stegosaurus*. But this battle never could have happened. *Stegosaurus* lived approximately 150 million years ago. Almost 80 million years passed before *Tyrannosaurus rex* came along. This means that you and *Tyrannosaurus rex* are closer together in time than the two dinosaurs. *Tyrannosaurus rex* was one of the last dinosaur species. It died out approximately 66 million years ago.

A Forest in Antarctica

Paleontologists have found dinosaur bones on every continent. *Spinosaurus* lived in what is now Africa, while *Tyrannosaurus rex* and *Stegosaurus* lived in North America. Dinosaurs even called Antarctica home. This frozen wasteland was not so cold back then. In fact the climate everywhere on Earth

Stegosaurus likely used plates on its back to keep cool. The plates may have helped disperse the dinosaur's body heat.

was much warmer than it is now. The continents also changed position during the time of the dinosaurs. They started out clumped together, and then they slowly moved apart.

Scientists know much of this through evidence they found in fossils and layers of rock. Fossils and rocks reveal not only what plants and animals lived long ago, but also information about Earth's climate and geography. Thanks to science, Earth's history and the dinosaurs did not disappear forever.

GIANTS

Many people are fascinated by giant dinosaurs. Museums showcase dinosaur skeletons with large teeth, long necks, and massive bodies. But not all dinosaurs were big. In fact, dinosaurs started out very small. The first dinosaur was probably the size of a pet Labrador retriever. It walked on two legs and likely ate insects. Over hundreds of millions of years, this creature evolved into all of the

Early dinosaurs, such as *Dilong*, were relatively small.

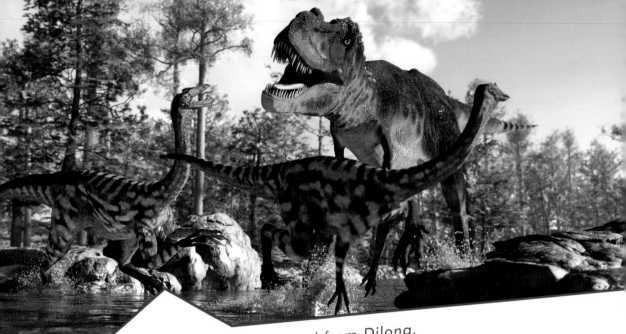

Tyrannosaurus rex evolved from Dilong.

different dinosaurs. Some stayed small. But others got gigantic. The science of evolution helps explain how this is possible.

Bigger Is Better

Evolution is all about change. When an animal has offspring, its body shape or behavior may be slightly different from those of its parents. If these changes help the animal survive, then it will probably pass them on to its own offspring. Over millions of years, many tiny changes add up to huge variations. A lot of dinosaur species evolved bigger and bigger bodies. For example, *Dilong* was a feathered dinosaur about the same size as a person. It lived approximately 138 million years ago in what is now China. One of *Dilong*'s many descendants was *Tyrannosaurus rex*. This giant's name means "King of the Tyrant Lizards." It was as long as a school bus and twice as tall.

Sauropod dinosaurs make *T. rex* look tiny. Sauropods were a group of giant plant-eating dinosaurs. The sauropod *Apatosaurus* likely weighed as much as

IN THE REAL WORLD
The Biggest Dinosaur Ever?

Paleontologists working in Argentina in 2014 dug up a huge leg bone. It measured 7.9 feet (2.4 m) long. The scientists found many other bones at the same site. The bones could belong to a new species of giant sauropod. Scientists estimate that it could have reached the length of a semitrailer and the weight of 14 elephants. It might have been the biggest dinosaur ever. But the giant does not have a name yet. The scientists who found it still have to prove that it really is a new dinosaur.

Monsters of the Sea and Sky

Many large creatures lived a long time ago. Not all of them were dinosaurs. Plesiosaurs were giants of the sea. They had flat bodies with four flippers. Some had extremely long necks. Pterosaurs flew through the sky. *Quetzalcoatlus* was the largest of this group of flying reptiles. Its outspread wings reached wider than the wings of an F-16 fighter jet. *Megalodon* was a humongous shark. One of its teeth was as long as an adult human's hand. But it never ate any dinosaurs, plesiosaurs, or pterosaurs. By the time *Megalodon* evolved, these other animals had already gone extinct.

five African elephants. Others grew longer than a blue whale or weighed as much as a whole herd of elephants. These dinosaurs had extremely long necks and tiny heads. If a person had the same shape, the person's head and neck would look like a peanut stuck at the end of a three-foot (1-m) straw. Evolution led to these big bodies and long necks, so these features must have helped sauropods survive. The long necks probably helped these dinosaurs reach leaves on tall trees. The large bodies likely

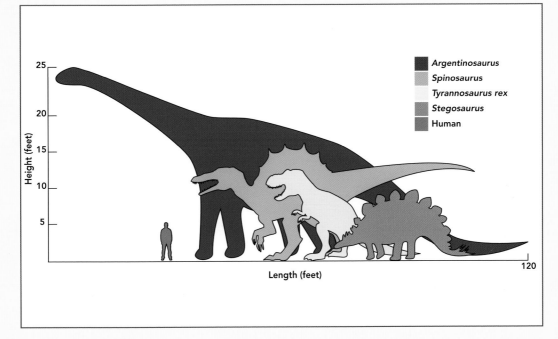

Dinosaur Sizes

Dinosaurs came in many shapes and sizes. *Argentinosaurus* is among the longest and heaviest dinosaurs ever discovered. The sauropod is estimated to have grown to 120 feet (37 m) long. How does the chart change how you understand how dinosaurs interacted?

kept them safe. It is not easy for a predator to hunt and kill an animal that is longer than a blue whale.

Sauropods' large size also had its drawbacks. Their giant bodies required massive amounts of food. Sauropods had to eat all day long. They had to swallow their food whole. If they chewed, they might not get enough to eat. They instead swallowed rocks

Paleontologists use knowledge of similar dinosaurs to learn about new ones.

along with whole leaves. The rocks helped mash up the leaves inside a special stomach called a gizzard.

Newborn dinosaurs were not whale-sized. All dinosaurs laid eggs. A newly hatched sauropod was approximately the size of a small goose. Female sauropods laid 15 to 40 eggs at a time. They likely piled plants on top of their nests to keep them warm. Sauropods were much too heavy to sit on such small eggs to keep them warm.

A Puzzle with Missing Pieces

Usually paleontologists do not find entire dinosaur skeletons. They may find just a few fossils, and some of them may be broken. Putting them together can be like working on a puzzle with lots of missing pieces. But scientists can learn a lot from just a few bones. For example, they can estimate the size of a whole dinosaur. To do this, they compare the lengths of the same bones on a similar dinosaur.

Of course, it's always best to find more pieces of the puzzle. Each new fossil discovery adds to the scientific knowledge about that type of dinosaur.

FURTHER EVIDENCE

Chapter Two talks about large dinosaurs, such as *Tyrannosaurus rex*. What is the main point of this chapter? Go to the article about the *T. rex* named Sue at the website below. Find a quote from the website that supports the chapter's main point.

A Dinosaur Named Sue

mycorelibrary.com/science-of-dinosaurs

CHAPTER THREE

FLIERS AND FIGHTERS

Some descendants of dinosaurs are still alive today. This may sound far-fetched, but it is true. Look out a window and wait for a bird to fly by. Birds may be small, but they have many traits that are similar to those of dinosaurs. For example, all birds have wishbones. This is a Y-shaped bone inside the chest. Theropod dinosaurs had wishbones too. *Tyrannosaurus rex*, *Velociraptor*, and *Spinosaurus* were

Similar to birds today, theropods, such as *Velociraptor*, relied on their hind legs to stand upright.

Birds with Teeth

Science has a very important rule: follow the evidence. Sometimes scientists think for a long time that a theory is true. But then they find new evidence that shows the theory was wrong. For example, *Archaeopteryx* was once known as the first bird. It had long feathers on its winglike arms. It also had teeth in its beak. It could probably fly, but not very well. Now scientists have found many more birdlike creatures. Some share even more traits with birds. *Archaeopteryx* may not be the first bird after all. In science a theory can always change based on new evidence.

all theropods. People, dogs, and other mammals do not have this bone. Many birds also have three forward-facing toes, as most theropods did.

Dinosaurs with Feathers

The first theropod dinosaur was a lizard-like running creature with teeth. Over hundreds of millions of years, this species evolved into feathered, beaked, flying birds. The change happened extremely slowly. Fossils show the link between dinosaurs and birds.

Scientists believe dinosaurs such as *Archaeopteryx* are linked to ancient theropods and modern birds.

In 2012 paleontologists in China discovered a trove of rare fossils. They found evidence of feathers, pressed into rocks. These fossils show that dinosaurs had feathers long before they could fly. *Yutyrannus huali*, a predator the size of a car, had short, fuzzy feathers. Some scientists think that all dinosaurs had feathers at one point. These plumes might have helped keep dinosaurs warm and attract mates.

Horns and Clubs

Dinosaurs evolved many interesting accessories, including pointy horns, giant frills, spiny backs, and clubbed tails. Many dinosaurs looked like they were

Dinosaur Sounds

What did dinosaurs sound like? A dinosaur called *Parasaurolophus* had a long, trombone-like structure rising up from the back of its head. The animal may have blown air through it to make noises. Scientists used an x-ray device called a CT scanner to take pictures of the inside of the structure. This way they did not have to cut open the fossil. Then they built a computer model. They had to guess what the soft parts of the dinosaur's nose and throat might have looked like. These parts of the dinosaur cannot fossilize. Finally they sent air through the model and recorded the resulting sound.

wearing weapons or armor. But did they really use their horns and spikes in battle? To answer that question, scientists look at animals today. Elk use their antlers to battle each other. The winner often gets a mate or territory. Rhinoceroses use their horns to scare off predators. Dinosaurs probably used their spikes and horns in similar ways.

But fighting is likely not the main purpose of some dinosaur spikes. Instead they may have made the dinosaur stand out among its own kind. For example, *Kosmoceratops*, a relative of *Triceratops,* had a total of 15 horns and spikes. It probably used them to attract a mate.

Other dinosaurs looked like walking tanks. *Ankylosaurus* and its relatives had bones inside their skin, forming thick armor. The knobby back of a crocodile has the same kind of bones. *Stegosaurus* had giant plates covering its back and a spiky tail. It likely used its spikes to swat at attackers. The plates may have helped the dinosaur attract mates.

EXPLORE ONLINE

Tyrannosaurus rex had tiny arms with two fingers each. But each hand actually had three finger bones. These bones still exist in birds' wings. *Oviraptor* was a species with feathers. It likely strutted like a peacock to show off its plumage. Can you find these two dinosaurs on the evolutionary tree on the website below? What else can you learn about how birds evolved?

A Family Tree
mycorelibrary.com/science-of-dinosaurs

CHAPTER FOUR

HUNTERS

Dinosaur science is about more than discovering and naming new creatures. Paleontologists also want to know how dinosaurs lived. Like all other animals, dinosaurs formed a community, called an ecosystem. Some hunted other dinosaurs. Others were wary of predators and ate plants, insects, or fish. Some darted and ran at the sight of predators, while others lumbered along slowly in herds.

Scientists look for evidence that tells them how dinosaurs lived.

IN THE REAL WORLD

High-Tech Fossil Hunting

Finding fossils typically requires a lot of luck. Experienced paleontologists know what kinds of rocks are most likely to contain fossils. But searching for those rocks takes time and effort. New technology can help. A team in Wyoming trained a computer to look for fossils. It found promising sites using images from satellites. A technology called ground-penetrating radar can peer through rocks. Scientists can use this technology to see rocks and fossils hidden underground.

Preserved dinosaur dung can reveal the foods they ate. Tooth marks on dinosaur bones can tell the story of a hunter's attack. Dinosaur footprints demonstrate whether a species lived alone or in packs. Dung, tooth marks, and footprints are called trace fossils. Trace fossils are records of dinosaurs' actions. Paleontologists find clues in the fossils. Then they use science and technology to paint a picture of dinosaur behavior.

Scientists found a *T. rex* tooth stuck in a duckbilled dinosaur's tail.

A Mighty Bite

Scientists have long known that *Tyrannosaurus rex* ate other dinosaurs. They have found broken bones in *T. rex* dung. They also have found bones with bite marks that appeared to match the teeth of the *T. rex*. But they could not prove that the giant animal was not a scavenger, a dinosaur that ate the meat of dead animals. In 2013 scientists were finally able to show that *T. rex* was a predator. They found a tailbone with a *T. rex* tooth stuck into it. The tissue around the tooth

A Giant Chicken

Tyrannosaurus rex had a skeleton very similar to that of a chicken. Scientists used a computer to build a virtual *T. rex*. They filled in the skeleton with muscles just like the ones found on a chicken, but much bigger. As an animal grows in size, it gets much heavier. It needs very bulky muscles to support the extra weight. The scientists learned that the *T. rex* could not run very fast. Its muscles could not have been strong enough for running.

had healed. This showed that the animal was alive when the *T. rex* bit its tail and that it lived through the attack.

The tyrant lizard king could swallow 500 pounds (227 kg) of meat in one bite. That is equal to approximately 2,000 hamburger patties. Its jaws snapped shut with incredible force. Scientists wanted to know how much force the dinosaur's jaws could generate.

So they made metal copies of *T. rex* teeth. Then they put them into a machine that could snap shut with different amounts of force. Using the machine, they made a bite pattern on cow bones that exactly

Velociraptors used their numbers to take down larger prey.

matched the one found on a *Triceratops* skeleton. It turns out that *T. rex* had the strongest bite of any land animal. It was ten times stronger than an alligator's.

Pack Attack

The movie *Jurassic Park* made *Velociraptor* famous. It depicts the dinosaur as a speedy, intelligent species that hunted in packs. *Velociraptor* was part of a group of dinosaurs with large brains. Because of this, some scientists believe it was one of the smartest dinosaurs. But its relative *Troodon* had a larger brain compared to its body size. It may have been as smart as some modern birds. *Troodon* also had longer legs, and it ran on its toes, making it better suited for fast speeds.

Scientists have found evidence that this group of dinosaurs hunted in packs. A close relative of *Velociraptor* and *Troodon* left footprints that showed at least six dinosaurs moving together. They may have been hunting. Elsewhere tracks have revealed the behavior of large plant-eaters. They show that sauropods most likely traveled in herds.

Hunting Giants

Sauropods may seem too big to be eaten. But a group of meat eaters called carnosaurs managed to hunt them. A set of tracks found in Texas tell the story of a carnosaur that chased and attacked a sauropod. Carnosaurs looked like *Tyrannosaurus rex*, and the two types of dinosaurs were related. But carnosaurs evolved first. *Giganotosaurus*, for example, was a carnosaur that grew even larger than *T. rex*. It was 46 feet (14 m) or more from head to tail and weighed approximately eight tons (7,260 kg).

In the 1800s, Mary Anning gained fame as a fossil hunter. At the time, women did not usually become scientists. In 1824 Lady Harriet Silvester wrote in her diary about a visit with Anning:

> *The extraordinary thing in this young woman is that she has made herself so thoroughly acquainted with the science that the moment she finds any bones she knows to what tribe they belong. She fixes the bones on a frame with cement and then makes drawings and has them engraved. . . . It is certainly a wonderful instance of divine favour— that this poor, ignorant girl should be so blessed, for by reading and application she has arrived to that degree of knowledge as to be in the habit of writing and talking with professors and other clever men on the subject, and they all acknowledge that she understands more of the science than anyone else in this kingdom.*
>
> Source: Hugh Torrens. "Mary Anning of Lyme (1799–1847): 'The Greatest Fossilist the World Ever Knew.'" British Journal for the History of Science 28.3 (1995): 265. Print.

Consider your Audience

The author of this text was surprised that a woman could be a skilled scientist, which was a common reaction at the time. Now women excel in science all the time. Rewrite this passage about Mary Anning for your classmates. How did your description of Anning's work change from the original?

CHAPTER FIVE

EXTINCTION

The mighty giants of the Mesozoic era are gone. What happened to them? Many people think that a giant rock from outer space, called an asteroid or meteor, hit Earth and wiped out the dinosaurs. This event is called a mass extinction. It marked the end of the Mesozoic era.

Not all scientists agree that a meteor was the only cause of the mass extinction. But there is evidence

The meteor that likely caused the dinosaurs' extinction left behind a crater that is 125 miles (200 km) wide.

Most meteors burn up as they enter Earth's atmosphere.

that a meteor struck Earth approximately 66 million years ago. There is also evidence that at this time more than half of all life on Earth died out.

Rise and Fall

The mass extinction did not affect every single dinosaur. Some dinosaurs had evolved into types of birds that survived. Other types of dinosaurs had already died out long before the meteor strike.

Extinction is a normal part of life on Earth. When changes happen in an environment or an ecosystem, animals need to change too. For example, if the weather gets warmer, bears may move farther north to a colder place. This type of change is called an adaptation. Adaptations sometimes lead to the evolution of a new species. If animals do not adapt or evolve, they may go extinct. Usually just a few species go extinct at a time. As some species fall, others rise to take their places.

A mass extinction is a rare event. An extreme change has to happen in the environment to kill off so many animals and plants.

IN THE REAL WORLD

The Return of the Dinosaurs

In the movie *Jurassic Park*, scientists bring dinosaurs back to life. The movie is not real, but some scientists are actually trying to do this. They are using genetics. This is a type of science that studies the code inside cells. This code, called DNA, carries instructions for how a living thing will look and behave. Scientists have tried to find dinosaur DNA inside fossils. But DNA is very delicate. Over millions of years, it breaks down. Scientists may never find actual dinosaur DNA. But they could try to recreate a dinosaur's genes using its close cousins: birds.

Animals unable to adapt to changes in their environment go extinct.

World on Fire

Imagine this: A *Triceratops* is eating grass when a giant rock darkens the sky and then slams into Earth. If the *Triceratops* survived the strike, then it was in for a difficult future. The meteor was approximately the size of a large city. It hit in the Yucatán peninsula in present-day Mexico. When it struck, it caused giant earthquakes

Meteor Watch

Could a meteor strike wipe out humans? Possibly. But people have a big advantage over dinosaurs. We have science. Astronomers are scientists who study outer space. They can see asteroids when they are very far away. If a giant asteroid were to come near Earth, astronomers could warn everyone. Space programs could then work to destroy the asteroid or move it away from Earth.

and tsunamis. Bits of hot dust and rock flew up into the air. The heat started fires. Smoke and dust filled the air until the sun disappeared. Plants cannot survive without the sun. When plants disappear, animals that eat those plants also die. Then the predators that hunt those animals die. The entire ecosystem falls apart.

There is evidence of increased volcanic activity near the time of the dinosaurs' mass extinction.

Scientists do not know if the mass extinction took days, months, or hundreds of years. Some think that the meteor was just one disaster among many. Scientists have found evidence that lots of volcanoes erupted near the time of the mass extinction. Some scientists think the increased volcanic activity was related to the meteor strike. These volcanoes spewed ash and gas into the air. This also could have led to many plant and animal deaths. In the same way that science has taught us about how dinosaurs lived, research could uncover more about their downfall.

Jack Horner is a paleontologist. He plans to change birds' DNA until they look like dinosaurs. He spoke about his plan in a speech in 2011:

> If you look at dinosaur hands, a Velociraptor has that cool-looking hand with the claws on it. . . . But as you can see, the pigeon, or a chicken . . . has kind of a weird-looking hand, because the hand is a wing. But the cool thing is that, if you look in the embryo, the hand . . . has the three fingers. . . . But a gene turns on that actually fuses those together. And so what we're looking for is that gene. We want to stop that gene from turning on, fusing those hands together, so we can get a chicken that hatches out with a three-fingered hand. . . . So what we're trying to do really is take our chicken, modify it and make the chickenosaurus. It's a cooler-looking chicken.
>
> Source: Jack Horner. "Building a Dinosaur from a Chicken." TED. TED, March 2011. Web. February 18, 2016.

Changing Minds

Is bringing dinosaurs to life a good idea? Take a side, and then imagine that your parents have the opposite opinion. Write a short essay to change their minds. Make sure you include facts and details that support your reasons.

FAST FACTS

- People who study dinosaurs are called paleontologists. They look at fossils to learn what dinosaurs looked like and how they lived.
- Dinosaurs roamed Earth for a very, very long time—185 million years. Scientists call this the Mesozoic era.
- Earth looked very different during the time of the dinosaurs. The continents started out in one big landmass called Pangaea and slowly moved to where they are now.
- The first dinosaur was probably approximately the size of a dog. Over time, dinosaurs evolved into many different species, including the biggest animals ever to walk on land.

- Half of the plants and animals on Earth died out approximately 66 million years ago. The dinosaurs were wiped out. Many scientists think that a meteor strike caused this mass extinction.
- Descendants of dinosaurs are still around today. Some birds survived the mass extinction and have evolved into today's birds.

STOP AND THINK

Why Do I Care?

Dinosaurs are not alive anymore, but the methods scientists use to learn about them matter for our lives today. Paleontologists look closely at tiny details to figure out what happened in the past. What evidence do you leave behind as you go through your day? What could a person learn about you from the things in your room or the items in your backpack?

You Are There

Chapter Two explains how dinosaurs evolved into giants. Imagine that you are a paleontologist, and you have just found bones that seem to be from the biggest dinosaur ever found. Write a newspaper article about your discovery. What will you name the new dinosaur? How do you know how big it was?

Dig Deeper

Chapter One introduces the Triassic, Jurassic, and Cretaceous periods. Many different dinosaurs lived in these periods, and they lived all over the world. Where and when did your favorite dinosaur live? With an adult's help, find reliable sources online. Write a paragraph about what you learned.

Take a Stand

Chapter Three talks about why dinosaurs had spikes, horns, and feathers. *Spinosaurus* was a huge dinosaur with a large sail-like structure on its back. What do you think this was for? Think about animals today that have similar features to help explain your ideas.

GLOSSARY

DNA
code inside cells that carries instructions for how a living thing will look and behave

fossil
evidence of a past life form

ecosystem
a community of plants and animals living in an environment

genetics
a branch of science that studies the DNA code inside cells

evolution
a slow process through which living things change and develop new forms and behaviors

paleontology
the science of studying ancient living things

extinct
when no members of a species remain alive

strata
layers of rock

LEARN MORE

Books

Holtz, Thomas R., and Luis V. Rey. *Dinosaurs: The Most Complete, Up-to-Date Encyclopedia for Dinosaur Lovers of All Ages.* New York: Random House, 2007.

Parker, Steve. *Dinosaurs: The Complete Guide to Dinosaurs.* Richmond Hill, ON: Firefly, 2009.

Petersen, Christine. *Fantastic Fossils.* Minneapolis, MN: Abdo, 2010.

Websites

To learn more about Super-Awesome Science, visit **booklinks.abdopublishing.com**. These links are routinely monitored and updated to provide the most current information available.

Visit **mycorelibrary.com** for free additional tools for teachers and students.

INDEX

ABOUT THE AUTHOR

Kathryn Hulick is a science writer and former Peace Corps volunteer who enjoys hiking, gardening, and painting. She has authored many books and articles for kids and lives in Massachusetts with her husband, son, and dog. Her favorite dinosaur is *Kosmoceratops*.